SPACE
STRUCK

PAIGE

LEWIS

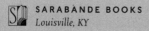
SARABANDE BOOKS
Louisville, KY

SPACE

Marie!
I'm so lucky
to exist in the
same universe
as you!

STRUCK

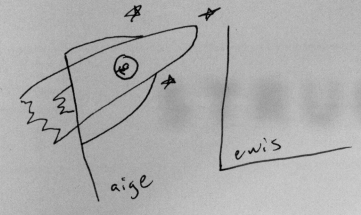

aige

Lewis

Library of Congress Cataloging-in-Publication Data

Names: Lewis, Paige, 1991– author.

Title: Space struck : poems / Paige Lewis.

Description: First edition. | Louisville, KY : Sarabande Books, 2019.

Identifiers: LCCN 2019006381 (print) | LCCN 2019009647 (e-book)

ISBN 9781946448453 (e-book) | ISBN 9781946448446 (pbk. : acid-free paper)

Classification: LCC PS3612.E973 (e-book) | LCC PS3612.E973 A6 2019 (print)

DDC 811/.6—dc23

LC record available at https://lccn.loc.gov/2019006381

Cover image © Joachim Bandau

Untitled, 2006

watercolour on paper

30 x 22.5 inches

Courtesy of the artist and Nicholas Metivier Gallery

Cover and interior design by Alban Fischer.

Manufactured in Canada.

This book is printed on acid-free paper.

Sarabande Books is a nonprofit literary organization.

 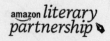

This project is supported in part by an award from the National Endowment for the Arts.
The Kentucky Arts Council, the state arts agency, supports Sarabande Books with
state tax dollars and federal funding from the National Endowment for the Arts.

for Kaveh

So while they journeyed up that sloping road,
the Sibyl told her story to Aeneas;
they exited the underworld at Cumae,
and there Aeneas offered customary
sacrifices, then landed on the shore
that, as yet, did not bear his nurse's name.

—OVID, *Metamorphoses*, Book XIV

I hear eternity
Is self-forgetting.

—LYNN XU, "Earth Light: I"

CONTENTS

III.

I

NORMAL EVERYDAY CREATURES

NORMAL EVERYDAY CREATURES

I'm going to show you some photos—
        extreme close-ups of normal, everyday
creatures. A patch of gray fur, half

a yellow eye. When you guess each creature
        right, you guess each creature into being.
Soon you'll have enough to open a zoo,

and people will visit because it's not every day
        they get to see everyday creatures in cages.
Oh, of course your zoo will have cages!

Otherwise you've just got world around you
        and who's going to pay for that? Your father?
Actually, let's not talk about fathers,

they are boring and offer clumsy advice
        on toothpick drawbridges, on soothing
saw grass wounds, on wearing the same pair

of underwear four days straight like the Boy Scouts.
        I was never a Boy Scout, though I did dream
of pinewood derbies and being afraid

of the forest. I might ask you one day to go
        camping, and if you have the desire to dance.
Please, when we finish spinning, aim me toward

the river. Once, while jumping from stone
        to stone, I slipped into the river and scared
a snake from his underwater hiding place,

and though he did not wisp his tongue at me,
        though he made no rude remarks about
my bony feet or the house I was raised in, I

wanted to harm him. I was frightened—
        I thought I knew where everything belonged.
I do know the snake does not belong in these

photos. It is not an everyday creature. I can tell
        you this because this is my game—I'm allowed
to give hints. And if, for some reason, you don't

belong in this space with me, getting fingerprints
        all over my glossy animals, then we'll journey
until we find the world in which we both fit.

And when the path grows too dark to see even
        the bright parts of me, have faith in the sound
of my voice. I'm here. I'm still the one leading.

ON THE TRAIN, A MAN
SNATCHES MY BOOK

On the train, a man snatches my book,
reads the last line, and says, *I completely get you,*

you're not that complex. He could be right—lately
all my *what ifs* are about breath: What if

a glassblower inhales at the wrong
moment? What if I'm drifting on a sailboat

and the wind stops? If he'd ask me how I'm
feeling, I'd give him the long version—I feel

as if I'm on the moon listening to the air hiss
out of my spacesuit, and I can't find the hole. I'm

the vice president of panic, and the president is
missing. Most nights, I calm myself by listing

animals still on the Least Concern end of the
extinction spectrum: aardvarks and blackbirds

are fine. Minnows thrive—though this brings
me no relief—they can swim through sludge

if they have to. I don't think I've ever written
the word *doom*, but nothing else fits.

Every experience seems both urgent and
unnatural—like right now, this train

is approaching the station where my beloved
is waiting to take me to the orchard, so we can

pay for the memory of having once, at dusk,
plucked real apples from real trees.

NO ONE CARES UNTIL YOU'RE
THE LAST OF SOMETHING

Someone squealed about the ivory-billed woodpecker
nesting on my back porch, and now there's a line

of binoculared men holding buckets of mealworms
and pushing their way into my home. I let them in

because I'd rather be host than hostage and really,
how could these lovers of redheaded grub-slurpers

be bad? They sport such splendid hiking shorts.
They press their noses against my sliding glass door

and ask for the woodpecker's name. I didn't give him
one—worried that if I named him, he'd never leave,

and honestly, I haven't been a fan since I watched
him raid a blue jay's nest for breakfast. Well, I didn't fully

watch—most of what I see, I see through the gaps
in my fingers. This sort of looking has turned me

boring—even the sun's been sighing, *Not you again,*
when it sees me. And I'm sure there's an alternate

universe where my gaze is unwavering, where I'm paid
to name the newest nail polish colors—Fiddlehead

Green, Feral Red, Geothermal Glitter—where
I don't hate documentarians for letting nature be

its gruesome self. But I'm stuck in this one, listening
to the demands of birdwatchers—they want postcards

and T-shirts, they want me to build an avian-themed
carousel in the middle of my living room. I want them

to leave. At midnight, I turn off the porch light,
and they swear they can still see inside his nest.

Someone asks, *Doesn't he look happy?*   *Yes,* they
all agree. *Don't you think he sounds like Fred Astaire*

with his tap-tap-tapping?   *Of course! Dresses like him, too.*
I don't know if it's the hunger, the heat, or the hours

of not blinking that turns them cultish, but I go with it.
I ask, *Shouldn't he have a break from your surveillance?*

They nod. *Yes, a break!* I'm giddy at the thought
of being alone. I say, *It's time to go home and rest.*

They remove their shoes and lie down on countertops,
in closets, and underneath my staircase. Wherever

there's space, they fill it—body against tired body—

pressed close as feathers.

SACCADIC
MASKING

—*a phenomenon where the brain blocks out blurred images*
created by movement of the eye

All constellations are organisms
and all organisms are divine
and unfixed. I am spending
my night in the kitchen. There
is blood in the batter—dark
strands stretch like vocal
cords telling me I am missing
so much with these blurred
visions: a syringe flick, the tremor
of my wrist—raised veins silked
green. I have seen the wings
of a purple finch wavering
around its body, stuck, burned
to the grill of my car, which means
I have failed to notice its flight—
a lesson on infinities, a lesson I
am trying to learn. I am trying.
Tell me, how do I steady my gaze
when everything I want is motion?

THE FOXES
ARE BACK

So this is water without your mouth-oil
        ghosting the surface. How much must I

swallow before I can say that the foxes
        are back, possessing our forest, asking,

Where are your fruits? And since you
        brought me the word *paradise,* I assume

they mean you. What else can I offer?
        That thing about boiling frogs isn't true—

they know what rising heat means
        and they will jump out. All my pots

are empty. Can you see the shroud
        of hunger, the crease between my

chest that says, *Fold here, Cut here?*
        Can't you see these pointed ribs want

to tangle—and what of my fruits?
        The foxes are lining my windows,

shielding their eyes from the lamplight
     with tiny-pawed soldier salutes. They scrape their

teeth against the glass—it almost
     sounds like chirping. It almost sounds

like you, skipping stones
     across our still-frozen pond.

BECAUSE THE COLOR
IS HALF THE TASTE

it's a shame to eat blackberries in the dark,
but that's exactly what I'm up to when a man

startles down the street screaming, *The fourth
dimension is not time!* He makes me feel stupid

and it's hard to sleep knowing so little
about everything, so I enroll in a night class

where I learn the universe is an arrow
without end and it asks only one question:

How dare you? I recite it in bed, *How dare
you? How dare you?* But still I can't find sleep.

So I go out where winter is and roll
around in the snow until a sharp rock

meets the vulnerable plush of my belly.
A little blood. Hunched over, I must look

like I'm hiding something I don't want to share.
And I suppose that's true—the sharp,

the warm wet. The color is half the pain. Why would anyone else want to see? How dare they?

THE MOMENT I SAW
A PELICAN DEVOUR

a seagull—wings swallowing wings—I learned
        that a miracle is anything that God forgot
                to forbid. So when you tell me that saints

are splintered into bone bits smaller than
        the freckles on your wrist and that each speck
                is sold to the rich, I know to marvel at this

and not the fact that these same saints are still
        wholly intact and fresh-faced in their Plexiglas
                tomb displays. We holy our own fragments

when we can—trepanation patients wear their
        skull spirals as amulets, mothers frame the dried
                foreskin of their firstborn, and I've seen you

swirl my name on your tongue like a thirst pebble.
        Still, I try to hold on to nothing for fear of being
                crushed by what can be taken because sometimes

not even our mouths belong to us. Listen, in
        the early 1920s, women were paid to paint radium
                onto watch dials so that men wouldn't have to ask

the time in dark alleys. They were told it was safe,
  told to lick their brushes into sharp points. These
    women painted their nails, their faces, and judged

whose skin shone brightest. They coated their
  teeth so their boyfriends could see their bites
    with the lights turned down. The miracle here

is not that these women swallowed light. It's that,
  when their skin dissolved and their jaws fell off,
    the Radium Corporation claimed they all died

from syphilis. It's that you're telling me about
  the dull slivers of dead saints, while these
    women are glowing beneath our feet.

WHEN I TELL MY BELOVED
I MISS THE SUN,

he knows what I really mean. He paints my name

across the floral bedsheet and ties the bottom corners
to my ankles. Then he paints another

for himself. We walk into town and play the shadow game,
saying, *Oh! I'm sorry for stepping on your*

shadow! and *Please be careful! My shadow is caught in the wheels
of your shopping cart.* It's all very polite.

Our shadows get dirty just like anyone's, so we take
them to the Laundromat—the one with

the 1996 Olympics–themed pinball machine—
and watch our shadows warm

against each other. We bring the shadow game home
and (this is my favorite part) when we

stretch our shadows across the bed, we get so tangled
my beloved grips his own wrist,

certain it's mine, and kisses it.

WHEN THEY
FIND THE ARK

Fox News buys exclusive broadcasting rights.
    My mother is sobbing, pressing her nails
    into my palm. She asks, *Is this live, is this live?*

When the men break their way into the ship, I swear
    I can smell a mixture of figs and lupines.
    The men don't need light. The ark is bright-

pulsing. Its floors are hay-dappled and wet-warped.
    Its stables—wide and filled with women.
    Women whipping around on all fours, their

heads pulled back, their mouths a frothed blur.
    Women sleeping straight-backed against
    wood beams, women speaking in trilling

chirps. My mother says, *This can't be the ark. Where
    are the bones? The men?* The men find
    one woman alone in her stable, curled

around an overturned bowl. The men lift her up.
    They lift the bowl, which gushes dust and
    dust. The women stop moving as the ark

fills, but the men want to save it, they don't want
        to see it dust-drowned. They throw the bowl
        out of the ark. Our TV goes black.

Outside, Lake Michigan is slopping up a thick
        gray paste, coating the stones. Inside,
        my mother replays the moments

before the cameras stopped. As the clouds press
        against our roof, she asks, *Don't you think
        the women running look a little like me?*

I LOVE THOSE WHO CAN WALK SLOW
OVER GLASS AND STILL KEEP

all their blood inside. I want to lick their smooth arches.
My beloved says he could walk over glass too—

It's all about weight displacement. He ruins
every illusion by staring at his own hands. I

ruin every illusion by threading it to hunger.
When Eric the Great was twelve, he ran away

to earn money for his family. He returned
to his mother, his pockets filled with coins,

and said, *Shake me, I'm magic.* So often our bodies
betray us. Just look at our feet, how they point

to what we desire. I don't notice mine until I'm
headed out the door—I get that from my parents.

My father, overgrown boy with a tight smile,
was always late, stopping to confirm his face

in every window's reflection. My mother was
a phone call saying *Go on and eat without me.*

The wind in this city is the cruelest, the kind
that searches for soft spots. Pulsing tender skulls.

I only know mirrors are silver because I've
seen one scuffed. All my spoons are weak-necked,

but I was wrong when I said the most desperate
sound was silverware clattering from a fast-pulled

drawer. Sometimes it's hard to tell the built from
the grown. Sometimes it's our fault. The serinette

was invented to teach canaries how to sing *correctly*.
When my beloved tells me I'm *correct* to love him, I

realize the sound isn't metal at all. It's not the coins rattling
on concrete, but the fingers scraping to pick them up.

As an adult, Eric the Great changed his name to Houdini
to honor Jean-Eugène Robert-Houdin, who would open his palms

to the audience and say, *Nothing here now—neither anything,*
nor anybody, before pulling his wife from the ether.

MY DEAR WOLFISH DREAMBOAT, STAND STILL

I don't want to alarm you,
but I'm pretty sure there are men

living on the surface of your eyes.
I can see them pairing up. Little

umlauts—fighting, maybe, or else
dancing. Do you think they know

life as you know it—as an arcade
where every good game is broken

and no one tells you, so you waste
token after token? Or would they

have more sense than that? I bet
these men love it most when you

get tired because they get tired,
too. When you press your palms

against your eyes, do they see
the sparks of light and create new

names for stars? Give them more.
Give them a moon—here, balance

this egg on your nose. Oh darling,
now they're building a telescope!

Do you think they can see me?
Clearly? Does it hurt?

II THE TERRE HAUTE PLANETARIUM
REJECTED MY PROPOSAL

THE TERRE HAUTE PLANETARIUM
REJECTED MY PROPOSAL

for more tactile audience participation.
And sure, their decision makes sense
if you consider the fact that no one likes

being pelted by meteorites, if you consider
the fact that I'm a miserable excuse for a planet.

Wildly rectangular orbit. I move
through life like I'm trying to
avoid a stranger's vacation photo.

Still, what do astronomers know
about public appeal? When naming

the color of our universe, they
had the chance to vote for either
Primordial Clam Chowder or

Cosmic Latte and they chose the latter.
Lately, I've been feeling betrayed by names:

the king cobra isn't a cobra, the electric
eel isn't an eel, and it turns out my anger
was fear all along.

I fear that I won't be respected until
I can sharp-whistle. I fear that I'll

come out the other side of rapture
with nothing but a taste for rapture,
no better than the plowboy prophet

who feared his words becoming
more dangerous than his hands.

Now, with my planetary hopes dashed,
I'm revising my lecture on futile repetition.
Imagine a line of identical circus clowns

frantically passing a pail of water from
the fire hydrant to their burning tent.

Now imagine a hole in the bottom
of that pail. Why would you imagine
such a thing? That tent was their home.

See, I'm afraid I'm not used to this
much control. I'm a miserable excuse

for a weapon. All stopped up with dread,
useless. I'm like a snake who, having
swallowed its fill of goose eggs, can

no longer escape through the gaps in the cage.
If I say, *Trust me*, you probably shouldn't.

Even I don't trust myself enough
to end on my own words. But trust me,
there are others who are powerfully worse,

who mold command into ammo, answers
into amnesia. I come from the same place

as everyone else, the place where
people take and the taking becomes
its own person. Where everyone hurts

and gets hurt, and the hurt can be heard
asking the same question—*Why isn't anybody*

stopping this? And the powerfully worse take
a vote, they elect their answer carefully:
Stopping what?

ON DISTANCE

It's nothing. The sun, with its plasma plumes
    and arching heat, is five million miles closer
        to Earth than it was in July, and we are still

alive. Today, I need you to stop thinking
    about such small numbers. Throw out your
        ruler. Your retractable yellow tape. Send that

blue egg back up to its nest unbroken. There
    is no way to tell how far it fell, so it never
        fell at all. No more contests. Make the dirt

spit its watermelon seeds back between
    children's teeth. Take the trophy buck
        from your father's house. He won't be

angry. I promise he won't come looking
    for it. Are you willing? What I mean is,
        in California, a city celebrates the life

of a firehouse light that's been burning
    for over a century. The citizens throw
        parades, they take photos, and they share

this light live through websites. What I mean
is, this one light can reach as many people
as the sun, and you only have to reach me.

GOD STOPS BY

to show me how healthy He's been. He's
sleeping more. He built his own gym.

Mostly muscle now, He gives me the fat
off his steak. I eat because He offers, not

because I need—it's hard to feel hungry
when everything in this world tastes small

and wrong, like rubber grapes or sun-boiled
eggs. When I was small, I was certain

that what was holy was mine—I caught
moths in the garden, pressed their wings

between my thickest book, and waited
for new moths to sprout up and out

of the pages. I ask God if He considers me
a cracked seed of grace. He says,

Yes, dear. I understand. It would be exhausting
to lead a life with careful consideration

for all things—stepping over anthills, saving
lizards from pools. I mean, if I was God enough

to be idolized, every statue would be a golden
depiction of me riding a goose-drawn chariot,

absentmindedly resting my shepherd's scythe
an inch away from their curved white

throats. Before God leaves, He clears the table,
pats my head, and presses two messages into

my palms. In my left, *You are the bridge.*
In my right, *You are the dust.*

WHERE I'M FROM, EVERY HOUSE IS A HOUSE WITH AN OBSTRUCTED VIEW

of the ocean. Oh, we are boring and superstitious
in my city. We believe tides are caused by millions of oysters
gasping in unison. Our rooms are eggshell white,
and our eggshells are poked through with silver spoons

to let the demons out. Yes, we fall in love,
but our love isn't golden so much as it is Midas lite—hard
and cheap—everything it touches turns green. We run
out of swoon quickly and respect the loveless, who are paid

to stand naked in department store windows, eating
homemade granola and sketching caricatures of anyone
who stops to stare. Yesterday, I gawked at a man
who wore a yellow knit cap on his penis. I was impressed

by how acutely aware he made me of my forehead,
which took up more than half of the portrait. I tipped him
generously with one hand and gave myself bangs
with the other. As a child, I was just as impatient and always

justly punished. When I tore the buds open in my
garden, I lost my garden. When I threw rocks into tree
branches to shake fruits loose, gravity was ruthless.
My new bangs do a marvelous job hiding those scars, but I

still miss the flowers. Where I'm from, we are practical
and ready to grow our mistakes. We whisper our heaviest
confessions into seed packets and launch them toward
the nearest planet, where they'll take root in neat rows—flower,

fruit, flower, fruit. This is how we build our new home.
How we make ourselves light enough for spaceflight. When
I arrive it will be easy to find which garden is mine.

YOU BE YOU, AND
I'LL BE BUSY

chewing five sticks of Juicy Fruit,
turning my jaw into a clicking, pain-

pricked mess and reaching for
another pack because hard work

is defined by a body's wreckage, and I
want you to know I'm hard at work

writing my presidential acceptance
speech: *A dartboard in every garage!*

A prison sentence for anyone caught
explaining magic. You be me, and I'll

be the man leaning against your fence,
expecting compliments on my new

haircut. Now, be you and take
this personality quiz. Do you scrape

your fork against your teeth? Results
are in: you're the kind of person

who has to stop doing that. You be
you, and I'll be racing across the yard,

trying to catch robins to prove how
tender I am with tender things. I'll be

Glenn Gould, hunched and humming
at your piano until it suddenly springs

a leak—the notes too full to hold
themselves together. I'll be me again

when I open the windows to keep
our apartment from flooding. Don't

be the woman on the sidewalk below,
drenched and furious. Instead, take

a turn as Gould. An older Gould—
wear gloves indoors, tell me you

can't have lovers for fear of harming
your elegant hands, clamber about the bed

being the man who always almost touches
me. Then become the man who does.

ST. FRANCIS
DISROBES

When Saint Francis materialized
in the corner of my studio apartment,
I figured I was in for a quick

message from the Almighty—*Thou
shalt lose weight,* or *Thou shalt not lie
with thine physics professor.* I thought

that it would take an hour—two hours
tops. On the first day, he didn't speak,
but held a steady rhythm of five sighs

per minute. On the second day, he moved,
began undoing his robe, and I
imagined red squirrels perched upon

high snag ribs and swallows—mouthy
little things—skimming the fields
of fabric around his ankles. In him,

I expected to find where the river
quirks, to learn how many feet
a millipede can live without. I

wanted to see my prayers tangled
in his chest hairs. Or maybe I
wanted no hair—for his body to be

bare as tonsured scalp, but now it's day
thirty and his hands are still unfolding
layers upon layers of brown wool.

Sometimes, I look past him to watch
infomercials, where hollow-cheeked
women shove apples into self-

cleaning juicers. I invite men over,
but they spend the night asking
questions he won't answer, like why

leaves in shadow appear light blue,
why bees prefer beer cans to daisies,
or why their wives don't forgive them

when they come home smelling of me?
I often dream of him speaking, of his
final unravel revealing a silk dress.

A present from my father, he says,
and as he raises his thumb to touch
my forehead I ask, *Which father?*

IN THE HANDS OF BORROWERS, OBJECTS ARE TWICE AS LIKELY TO BREAK

I.

Build me a house with so many rooms

we'll have to plan where we lie
days in advance. Such joy in naming:

Analemma Room, Room of Caviar
and Unbearable Situations, Room

Where We Spontaneously Combust.
That'll be my favorite, where we

breathe in our own rising heat, where
our water evaporates and returns

as condensation on the windowpane.

II.

My ghost drops by so often
I no longer feel obligated to offer

it our good coffee. Halfway through
my second mug, a roach leg surfaces

like a rotting mast. *I'm so tired,*
it says. *I'm so tired and I don't trust*

what the world is up to with its fat horses
and its pupils sewn into place. I hear

I love you and keep drinking.

III.

I'm so close to tired.

Every man I meet dreams
of fucking me in star-clotted fields.

It's selfish to want to witness awe—
to stand in a museum and shift

your gaze between the painting
and your reflection in its frame.

IV.

More than anything, I want
the ability to respond perfectly

to tragedy—like when you said
you didn't enjoy the sound of my

voice, I should have sung louder
because, my little pocket of pearls,

my God-dodging bumper crop
of brown hair, you can't cut off

a piece of the sacred and not expect
ruin: halos mutate into pipe cleaners,

galaxies into falling matches.

TURN ME OVER, I'M DONE ON THIS SIDE

I'm almost positive I've got what it takes to become a saint
      because I've stopped breaking what I can't afford,
        and if I look up for long enough, everyone looks up.
Are there any lemmings that refuse to mate because they

know that the overcrowding of their burrows and the sound
      of a thousand offspring scritching up the tunnels will
        drive them, panicked, off cliffs and into the ocean?
Little rodent virgin saints. It's the same with us—scientists

in the '70s predicted that by the year 2000 we'd be living
      off kelp. We take so much from the sea. In Italy,
        the last known sea silk weaver prays while she turns
mollusk spit into golden thread—*The sea has its own soul,*

and you have to ask permission to take a piece of it. She's
      a saint without even wanting to be, and here I am
        stuffing plastic diamonds up my nose and waiting
in the park for joggers to notice my light-reflecting breath.

I believe those who believe that the greatest comedians
      are the ones who've suffered most. Saint Lawrence
        cracked jokes while being roasted alive. There
were so many storms the year I turned five, I forgot what

our windows looked like unboarded. After Hurricane Andrew,
        I watched from the porch as my brother canoed into
        a downed wire. I wonder if we name storms because
naming is the only power we're left with. Give me more time

and I'm sure I could make this funny. Recently, people learned
        that prayers reach heaven fastest by balloon. The party
        stores have turned into churches, and I can't afford
the inflated prices. Was that a good joke? Maybe I could

be a saint after all. I just hope I'm forgiven for the nights I
        spend on the fire escape, untying this city's prayers
        long enough to hear the first few words. Each one
starts the same—*Make this mine, Lord. Make this mine.*

GOLDEN
RECORD

We know nothing about your bodies, but we want to
teach you ours. We aren't weak. Our skeletons

are built to stand even when certain parts break
or go missing. And while most of us are born

with collarbones, there are some who aren't—
in the '80s they made a living rescuing children

from wells. On this planet, you have to be useful
to be kept around. Our interests include improving

the aesthetic appeal of practical tools—
cat-eared umbrellas, musical toilets, red bridges.

Our main turnoff is nature, though we find ways
around it. For instance, with the right mix

of chemicals and a lot of patience, we can change
a chicken egg into a single-use camera. How advanced

are you? We're not looking to move backward—
even our primal yelps crawl up the throat

and out the mouth—but we're known to be flexible
in tight situations, we're known to be honest

when desperate, and honestly,
we're right here, if you like what you see.

CHAPEL OF THE
GREEN LORD

This spring, the smog is so thick
I can't see the stars, which means
there aren't any stars left. It's pointless

     to argue against this, to say,
     no they're on vacation, no
     they'll come back with new summer
     hats and an answer

to my question: If this world
is a plucked violin string, am I part
of its sound or its stillness?

     Once, I woke and believed myself full
     of the old heaven. I wanted to trap it,
     make it stay. I swallowed
     a hive's worth of honey, and—

and still, no stars. This smog
is thick enough to turn my lungs gummy.
I stay inside, line my bed

with spider plants and succulents,
christen it Chapel of the Green Lord,
and go to sleep with the sheets pulled up
over my sticky mouth.

DIORAMA OF GHOSTS

i spent years living with ghosts
strung between my teeth

Like corn silk?

like ghosts

How did they get there?

good hygiene or poor
taste
perhaps a blend

Why keep them?

i was so sad
i would have harbored
anything

*Have you earned the right
to say sad?*

i dont want to
talk about that

When did they leave?

all at once

. . .

they cannonballed
right into a punch bowl
and ruined my best
shirt

Do you know why they left?

when the dust is swept
the broom is stored
behind the door again

                           Do you miss them?

they made me the delicate
gulper i am today

                           But do you miss them?

the mention
of silence

                           I don't understand.

worse
than the silence itself

SPACE
STRUCK

Ann Hodges, the first confirmed meteorite victim

I remember the doctor lifting my nightgown
to see how high the bruise climbed. He seemed

disappointed—*A thinner woman would've died.* I was
small when I was young. Didn't take up much space.

In fact, I could fit all of me in a suitcase until I
was sixteen, and maybe I was dreaming of this

when the stone hit and I woke to light streaming
through the ceiling. I think I thought it was God,

since I'd been told it's painful to bear witness.
At any rate, it was a blessing to my husband,

who pretends the bruise is still there. At night,
he lifts my nightgown and kneads my thigh.

He says, *How deep,* like he's reaching into a galaxy.
He says, *How full,* and looks up to see if I wince.

III

YOU CAN TAKE OFF YOUR SWEATER,
I'VE MADE TODAY WARM

Sit on the park bench and chew this mint leaf.
Right now, way above your head, two men

floating in a rocket ship are ignoring their
delicate experiments, their buttons flashing

red. Watching you chew your mint, the men
forget about their gritty toothpaste, about

their fingers, numb from lack of gravity.
They see you and, for the first time since

liftoff, think *home*. When they were boys
they were gentle. And smart. One could

tie string around a fly without cinching it
in half. One wrote tales of sailors who

drowned after mistaking the backs of
whales for islands. Does it matter which

man is which? They just quit their mission
for you. They're on their way down. You'll

take both men—a winter husband, and
a summer husband. Does it matter which

is—don't slump like that. Get up, we have
so much work to do before—   wait   you're going

the wrong   way   small whelp of a woman!   this is not

          how we   behave   where are you going

                                   this world is already   willing

to give you anything   do you want to know Latin

                                        okay   now everyone

here knows Latin   want inflatable   deer

                    deer!   I promise the winter/

summer children will barely hurt   dear   I'm hurt

that you would ever think

                    i don't glisten to you   i'm always glistening

tame your voice   and   turn around

the men are coming   they've traded everything for you the gemmy   starlight

the click   click   click

                                          of the universe   expanding

                        stop

            aren't you known   aren't you
                                              known here

how can you be certain that anywhere else will provide

                                          more pears than you could ever eat

            remember the sweet rot of it all

come back   you forgot your sweater

what if there's nothing there when you—

            you don't have your
                                    sweater

                                          what if it's cold

I'VE BEEN TRYING TO FEEL
BAD FOR EVERYONE

I'm learning that a miracle isn't a miracle
without sacrifice, because when the birds
brought manna, we ate the birds. I'm learning

that we forgive those we know the least,
like when my brother had another episode
and stabbed his wife, I said to my beloved,

disorder, genetic, and he never yelled at me
again. Lord, teach me patience, for every fruit
I've ever picked has been unripe. Teach trust

that reaches past an opened and unwatched
purse. Lord, I've seen painted depictions
of an infant Christ winding toy helicopters.

I know it isn't always about suffering, so send
us a good flood. Deliver a nectar that will soften
fists and lift these red stains from our doorframes.

THE RIVER REFLECTS
NOTHING

This morning I watched a neighborhood
boy throw his model plane into the air

with his right hand and shoot it down
with the garden hose in his left. My

hands were never that quick. When
my mother lived by the river, I lived

by the river. I knelt over it with legs red
and pebble-dented. Reaching in, I pulled

back empty fists and it always seemed
like a trick, those tadpoles all green-glinting

and shadows. My brother could catch
them, could make the squirming real

in his palm before he swallowed each whole.
We are only remembered as cruel when

what we harm does not die quickly. I
don't know how long it took the tadpoles,

but I know I was trying to say I'm sorry
when I leaned down, pressed my mouth

against his stomach and said, *If you'd*
just let me catch you, I'd let you go.

LAST NIGHT I DREAMED
I MADE MYSELF

your paperweight. This seems
wrong. Seems like a sign that I need
to spend more time on my own, so I

call my friend and drive him to the store
full of overpriced healing stones. I want
the women shopping to know I'm not

with my friend. I want them to know
how great I'm doing with my adventures
in independence. I'm ready to shout,

Look at my healthy new life! But my friend
thinks it's a bad idea to frighten people
in a place with so many hard throwables.

Would they hurt me? These women
look as if they'd smell like pink magnolias
and violin rosin if I got close enough,

but I won't. I'm too busy searching for
the stone that best represents me—it's
not the blue one specked with God bits,

or the ear-shaped obsidian. It's
not anything polished—and I think
about how hard it is for me to believe

in the first Adam because if Adam
had the power to name everything,
everything would be named Adam.

Then I think, *That's a pretty smart thought.*
I don't say it to my friend. I don't say it
to the magnolia women. Do they still

count, these hours I've spent on my
own? Do they still count if I'm saving
all of my shiniest thoughts for you?

GOD'S SECRETARY, OVERWORKED

Get real, darling. If He answered all prayers
you'd be dead five times over. And I don't
mean the men you left just wished you were
gone, I mean they scraped holes in your photos

and kneeled in front of votive candles, begging
for you to sleep between the tracks and train.
One even asked for you to appear in his bed
still wet from the lake. And while I'm not one to name

names, you should be grateful that God
doesn't work like that. Listen, I've got children
in car wrecks and old folks in hospice to call on,
but take my advice and stop asking for men's

forgiveness. It's a dangerous demonstration.
If you offer a sorry mouth, they'll break it.

PAVLOV WAS THE
SON OF A PRIEST

which is a biographical fact only ever stated
when discussing a man of either unrivaled
righteousness or extreme wickedness.

Imagine this: he never once used a bell
in his saliva experiments, unless you count
the plink of kibble falling from his dogs'

surgically opened throats, and why would
you count that? I admit I often tell you
about the cruelties of others to stifle

the growling in my own troubled core. I
sense something is about to happen, though
I can't tell you what because last night,

after I prophesized that a man would steal
the Smithsonian's rare and hideous pumpkin
diamonds, I had no fun at all crouching

behind the museum's display cases until
the night guard carried us out by our ears.
She told you, *Treat your mouth less*

like a garbage chute. She told me, *Forget*
what you think you know about space. But I
only really know about its violence. I forget

that the moon smells like spent gunpowder.
I forget what would happen to your body
in a black hole. I don't forget your body.

This would be unforgivable, and I have
so many strikes against me already. I'm sorry
I couldn't hide my joy when you said *lonely*.

It made me feel useful. I used to be aimless—
swallowing marbles and clicking my way
through cities, licking my thumbs to smooth

the eyebrows of almost any man. Now, I
demand a love that is stupid and beautiful,
like a pilot turning off her engines midflight

to listen for rain on wings. I want to find
you a peach so ripe that even your breath
would bruise it. I want to press its velvet

heat against your cheek, make you edge
into the bite until your mouth is too wet
to ask questions. If something happens,

let it. I admit I couldn't hear the thief's
footsteps over the museum alarm, but
I'm certain that if the diamonds jostling

against ugly diamonds in his drawstring
bag sounded like anything, they sounded
like bells.

DIORAMA OF OUR NEED TO
ESCAPE THE COLD WE MAKE

My beloved steadies my balance on the outer wall
of the zoo. He says that even in their sleep, captive giraffes
    know they're captive—*They don't make that midnight hum*

    in the wild. He wants to connect these stemmy-necked
        leopards to my crooning, but it's only noon. He reaches
        up, pokes his finger through the sun, and spirals it into

an apple's dizzy peel. Now red. Now waxy. He
ribbons it through his lips. *See,* he says. His singed
    mouth. *We've grown so big. It's time we got out of here.*

    I don't want *out*, but I do grow cold, and the cold
        comes strong—and the dark. The streetlights
        are stubborn here—they decide when to light,

it will not be decided for them. The humming swells
so loud I can only focus on everything my beloved is not.
    He is not me from the future—his pockets aren't

    filled with space dust. He is not God—he still needs
        my help unsnagging his hair from jacket zippers.
        Where are we going? He rips a hole into the side

of the wall. He squeezes my hand, leading me in
through the hollow and out beside a mountain, which
    has only us to confide in. It says, *I am very thin*

    and not fit to hold you. We climb it anyway. The mountain
        teeters and falls back, flattening the town below.
        My beloved calls it An Exceptional Wreck. He feeds flint

to a hawk and sends it sparking over the fields. I don't
understand his bigness, or his dreamy definition of guilt,
    and I don't argue. I used up my toothiness years ago—

    rendered myself kind. And besides, he's teaching me
        confinement. How to feel the fences. When he
        pulls me toward the fire, he pulls me by my wrist.

MAGIC
SHOW

The magician pulls handkerchiefs from her throat
until the rope of knotted silk ends, and she—

she keeps going, her tongue pressed down
to make room for what comes next: swords,
of course, each one longer than the one before.

Then a live Doberman that limps offstage, soaked
and shivering. For a moment, the magician's parted lips

reveal only darkness, but she reaches in and brings
forth a crystal chandelier with its candles still lit.
I watch for years, surviving off what she coughs up:

pheasants and scalloped potatoes on silver trays,
deboned salmon slabs. I'm not sure if her belly

shrinks because she takes everything out, or
because she lets nothing in, but I'm grateful for her
dedication. For the pastel Easter basket, the kettle

of hawks instead of white doves, the fishbowl
and ceramic scuba diver who stands atop glow-

in-the-dark rocks, for the pay phone, the umbrellas,
ribbed and open, the top layer of frozen lake,
and the ice skates. For the twinkling music box,

and the green sweater I thought I'd lost in Michigan.
For the mattress and box spring I'm grateful,

though I'm the last one in the audience, and I
have seen enough. I tell her to stop, and she stops.
As she packs, I ask about the first object she ever

lifted from her mouth. She opens her traveling case
and shows me the jar of wisdom teeth she keeps

nestled between sequined vests. And this makes
sense, like how Earth refuses to release its pull
on the moon. *Look,* she says, *look how full I was.*

SO YOU WANT TO
LEAVE PURGATORY

Here, take this knife. Walk down
the road until you come across

a red calf in its pasture. It will
run toward you with a rope tied

around its neck. Climb over
the fence. Hold the rope like a leash.

You haven't eaten in years. Think—
are you being tested? Yes, everything

here is a test. Stop baring teeth
upon teeth and leave the calf

to its grazing. Lift your arms toward
the sky and receive nothing. Keep

walking and think about the rope
around that calf's neck. Consider

how fast its throat will be choked
by its own growing. Walk until you

understand what the knife was for.

Now forget it. Here, take this knife.

ROYAL I

My specific heart, know that I am king here.
    I have my sword, my seat, and my passions
        pinned to the royal bulletin board for all
            to see. I'm a kind king, no skink's ever shed

his blue tail in fear of me. I perform my tasks
    bravely—just yesterday I sewed the flappy
        lakes into place without thimble or worry
            of prick. I've granted everyone the freedom

to eat dinner in bed, and I've rid the realm
    of rats by reading their tiny diaries out loud
        until they ran into the forests, red-cheeked
            and babbling. I'm understandably busy,

so if I decide I no longer have time or want
    for children, I expect an *Alright, your brightness,*
        and for you to stop building our miniatures
            out of pipe cleaners and meltwater. I'm kind.

I'm making love easy for everyone. It feels
    exactly as the movies proclaimed. As king,
        it's my duty to be one with the universe,
            but I hate how the galaxies hover over me,

expecting mistakes. And, my love, I might
      make a few. It's essential for me to trust, to tell
            you that, if I lose my calm—if there comes a day
                  where I walk into a room and everyone finds

a corner to hide in, I'll need you to be ready to
      de-thorn the throne. My weaknesses are many
            and stubborn. If you must strike, do so at night,
                when I'm outside and alone and looking up.

NOTES

NOTES

The first line of "Saccadic Masking" comes from Coulson Turnbull's *Life and Teachings of Giordano Bruno* (Gnostic Press, 1913).

The title "You Be You, and I'll Be Busy" is inspired by the title of the poem "I'll Be Me and You Be Goethe" by Heather Christle, which can be found in her collection *What Is Amazing* (Wesleyan, 2012).

In "Diorama of Ghosts," the lines "when the dust is swept / the broom is stored / behind the door again" come from Saint Bernadette Soubirous who said, "The Virgin used me as a broom to remove the dust. When the work is done, the broom is put behind the door again."

The firehouse light mentioned in "On Distance" is known as the Centennial Light. It is located in Livermore, California.

The final line of "God Stops By" comes from Rabbi Simcha Bunim Bonhart of Przysucha. One of his famous teachings is about how everyone should carry two notes with them. One note should read, "For my sake was the world created," while the other note should read, "I am but dust and ashes."

In "Turn Me Over, I'm Done on This Side," the lines *"The sea has its own soul, / and you have to ask permission to take a piece of it"* come from Chiara Vigo, the last sea silk weaver. In a 2015 BBC News Magazine interview with Max Paradiso, Vigo says, "The sea has its own soul and you have to ask for permission to get a piece of it."

In "I've Been Trying to Feel Bad for Everyone," the painting referenced is *The Virgin and Child with Saint Benedict* from the Priory of St. Hippolytus of Vivoin. It's located at the Musée de Tesse in Le Mans, France.

"God's Secretary, Overworked" is inspired by the poem "The Frustrated Angel" by Jay Hopler, which is included in his book *Green Squall* (Yale, 2006).

ACKNOWLEDGMENTS

I would like to thank the editors of the following publications where these poems first appeared, often in earlier versions:

Adroit Journal: "Diorama of Ghosts"

American Poetry Review: "I Love Those Who Can Walk Slow Over Glass and Still Keep," "In the Hands of Borrowers, Objects Are Twice as Likely to Break"

Black Warrior Review: "Royal I"

Colorado Review: "I've Been Trying to Feel Bad for Everyone"

decomP: "Magic Show"

DIAGRAM: "Saccadic Masking"

Florida Review: "God's Secretary, Overworked"

Indiana Review: "So You Want to Leave Purgatory"

The Journal: "Turn Me Over, I'm Done on This Side"

Los Angeles Review of Books: "You Be You, and I'll Be Busy," "No One Cares Until You're the Last of Something"

Muzzle Magazine: "St. Francis Disrobes"

Ninth Letter: "The River Reflects Nothing"

Passages North: "When They Find the Ark"

Pleiades: "Diorama of Our Need to Escape the Cold We Make"

Ploughshares: "Pavlov Was the Son of a Priest"

Poetry: "You Can Take Off Your Sweater, I've Made Today Warm"

Academy of American Poets' *Poem-a-Day*: "When I Tell My Beloved I Miss the Sun,"

Redivider: "On Distance," "My Dear Wolfish Dreamboat, Stand Still"

The Shallow Ends: "The Foxes Are Back"

Sixth Finch: "The Moment I Saw a Pelican Devour"

Sugar House Review: "Space Struck"

TriQuarterly: "Last Night I Dreamed I Made Myself"

Waxwing: "Where I'm From, Every House Is a House with an Obstructed View," "Golden Record"

Oceans of gratitude to Hanif Abdurraqib, Eloisa Amezcua, Madiha Jamil Baksh, Ruth Baumann, Chase Berggrun, Paige Blair, Kelly Butler, Damian Caudill, Sumita Chakraborty, Marianne Chan, Cortney Lamar Charleston, Heather Christle, Tiana Clark, Eduardo C. Corral, Christopher DeWeese, Andrew Epstein, Kat Finch, Joseph Gordon, Barbara Hamby, Jay Hopler, Heather Hughes, Sara Eliza Johnson, James Kimbrell, David Kirby, Zach Linge, Carly Joy Miller, Aimee Nezhukumatathil, Dustin Pearson, Katherine Riegel, Jayme Ringleb, Don Share, Nomi Stone, Melissa Studdard, John Taylor, Leah Umansky, R. A. Villanueva, and Jane Wong for their guidance, inspiration, and support.

More oceans to the Sarabande team—Sarah Gorham, Kristen Miller, Danika Isdahl, and Joanna Englert—for making this dream book a reality.

And even more oceans to my family—Mary, Raychel, Richard, Patrick, and Stefanie—for everything.

Love and love and love to my husband, favorite poet, and bright particular, Kaveh Akbar.

KAVEH AKBAR

PAIGE LEWIS's poems have appeared in *Poetry, American Poetry Review, Ploughshares,* and elsewhere. They teach at Purdue University and in the low-residency MFA program at Randolph College.

SARABANDE BOOKS is a nonprofit literary press located in Louisville, KY. Founded in 1994 to champion poetry, short fiction, and essay, we are committed to creating lasting editions that honor exceptional writing. For more information, please visit sarabandebooks.org.